THE LITTLE BOOK OF POKER TIPS

PETER FRENCH

THE LITTLE BOOK OF POKER TIPS

PETER FRENCH

A.
Absolute Press

First published in Great Britain in 2006 by
Absolute Press
Scarborough House, 29 James Street West
Bath BA1 2BT, England
Phone 44 (0) 1225 316013 **Fax** 44 (0) 1225 445836
E-mail info@absolutepress.co.uk
Web www.absolutepress.co.uk

Reprinted 2010

A catalogue record of this book is available from the British Library

ISBN 13: 9781904573500

Printed and bound in Malta on behalf of Latitude Press

‘Life consists not in holding good cards
but in playing those you hold well.’

Josh Billings
(1818–1885)

1

In any form of poker,

only enter a pot with a decent starting hand.

More money is lost at poker through the contravention of this basic strategy than by any other means. Resolve that you will never again waste good money on weak starting hands, no matter how often you see someone else getting lucky with them.

2

Pick the weakest game

you can possibly find

at your level.

This is especially true online. Don't just dive in – look for a game where you can see that there are people who don't know what they're doing. There are plenty of them.

3

Be patient.

Patience is an absolutely key poker requirement. No matter what game you're playing, you will go for long periods of time without getting a playable hand. You must be prepared for this, and resist at all costs the temptation to play a sub-standard hand on the grounds that it's the best one you've seen for an hour.

4

In Draw Poker, never enter the pot with less than a pair of Jacks,

and in first or second position only call with Aces or better. And never keep a kicker with a pair in Draw Poker.

5

Never call a raise in Draw Poker with less than two pairs, Jacks up.

Half of all two pair hands are Jacks up or better, so if you call a raise with less than this you are taking a big risk.

6

Occasionally bluff at Draw Poker by standing pat,

but don't do it with absolutely nothing. Two small pairs is a good hand to try it with – you may still win even if you are called, and the worst that can happen is that you lose but get some free advertising for your bluff. This may help you get callers the next time you have a genuinely big hand.

7

At low-limit Hold'em, it's usually correct to **bet your monster hands** rather than slow-play them. Slow-playing huge hands is so common at the lower limits that the other players will probably not put you on the hand that you actually hold.

8

Play middle and low pairs very carefully at Hold'em.

Do not call big pre-flop raises with them, and if you don't hit trips on the flop, fold immediately in the face of a bet.

9

Aim to **play your drawing hands against lots of opponents.** This is because although the odds are probably against you making your hand, on the occasions you do hit you want as many players in the pot as possible to pay you off.

10

In Hold'em, position is a vital part of the game, often ignored by beginners. Pay careful attention to your position at all times. Money moves in a clockwise direction round a Hold'em table. The earlier your position, the better a starting hand you need to enter the pot.

11

Remember that

the best position in Hold'em is on the button.

This is because you will always be last to act after the flop and in subsequent betting rounds, giving you the huge advantage of seeing what your opponents have done before you have to make your decision. You can't win every hand from the button, but you should never waste the opportunities it presents.

12

Beware players who flat-call under the gun

(first to act). Most Hold'em players know that you need a premium hand to enter a pot from first position, and if you find yourself facing an opponent post-flop who limped in from there, you should put him on a big starting hand.

13

If you're holding a straight at Hold'em, but the bottom card is in your hand rather than on the board – beware. The chances of someone else holding a higher straight are so high that it's not worth risking any chips on it.

14

Never slow-play AA or KK before the flop.

If you don't raise, the chances of your rockets or cowboys being beaten go up and up. Occasionally everyone will fold, but that's a chance you have to take. Better that than to be beaten by 8-7 suited or something equally horrible.

15

Don't let the fact that your hole cards are suited at Hold'em unduly influence your decision whether to fold or not.

Most low-limit players place far too much value on suited cards. The fact that your 5-4 is suited does not make it playable. You are 8/1 to catch a flush draw, let alone the actual flush, which may very well be beaten by a higher flush anyway!

16

Always fold a drawing hand against a single opponent. The odds are never good enough against one player to justify chasing a flush or straight draw.

17

Note that the average hand when you're playing heads-up (i.e. against a single opponent) is Q7.

Hold'em is an aggressive game, but never more so than when you're heads-up. Raise pre-flop with any hand better than Q7, but be prepared to get away from the hand if your opponent re-raises.

18

Play in lots of online tournaments,

especially Sit 'n' Gos. You know in advance how much you can lose, so they provide a wonderful opportunity to play lots of poker hands and practise your skills at length with the absolute minimum of risk.

19

Watch the board. Always be aware of what hands would beat you if combined with the flop, and assess the chances of someone holding such a hand.

20

Weak Aces

(Ace with a kicker below Ten) are called that for a reason. Become a better player:

fold them instantly, before the flop at a full Hold'em table.

21

If you've raised before the flop,

and got callers but no re-raisers, you should generally represent the flop whether it has hit your hand or not. Unless you are at a very loose table, the other players will have to have enormous hands to call you.

22

When you are on the button in Hold'em, or even one position behind the button, always **consider trying to steal the blinds.** There are plenty of very cautious players who will fold almost anything in the face of a raise. You can always back off if one of the blinds comes back over the top at you.

23

Odds are important in all forms of poker. Take some time to learn at least the ones that come up most often. For example, the odds of filling a flush with two cards to come are slightly better than 2/1; with just one card, they are slightly worse than 4/1.

24

To work out the percentage **possibility of hitting your draw at Hold'em,** multiply the number of outs by the number of cards still to come, and then double the total.

25

At a full Hold'em table, the odds on being dealt a pair or an Ace are 4/1. This means that on average, two players in every hand will hold either an Ace or a pair. This is **worth remembering when you are considering calling a raise** with a hand inferior to either of these.

26

The odds of filling an inside straight with one card are nearly 11/1. This means it is almost never correct to make this draw. It's the oldest saying in poker, with good reason:

never draw to an inside straight.

27

Beware AQ, AJ and A10 in No-Limit Hold'em.

Over and over again weak players get busted out of tournaments by AK, AA or KK with these hands. Don't call a big pre-flop raise with them.

28

Although it's correct to play aggressively **towards the end of a tournament,** never risk your whole stack unless you are an overwhelming favourite to win. For example, it's quite wrong to go all-in with a pair (other than Aces or Kings) before the flop. The chances of someone calling you with one or two overcards, and then hitting a pair by the river are far too great.

29

Don't call a pre-flop raise unless

you have a raising hand yourself, especially at No-Limit Hold'em. This is one of the quickest fixes for most beginner and intermediate poker players. And always consider re-raising rather than just calling. You have a better chance of taking control of the hand.

30

Watch for betting patterns

in your opponents at No-Limit Hold'em. For example, if you can identify that a particular player always bets one amount when he's got a moderate hand, but a different amount when he's got a premium hand, you can use that knowledge to decide when to play against him and when to fold.

31

In No-limit Hold'em, a raise of 5 times the big blind is usually enough to **eliminate most of the field before the flop.** At low limits, any less than this will frequently attract two or three callers, or even more.

32

In the early stages of online Sit 'n' Go No-Limit Hold'em tournaments,

go all-in before the flop with pocket Aces or Kings. The odds are very high that you will get a caller with a weaker hand, and double up your stack.

33

Set yourself a realistic target

before every session of poker you play.
If you're just playing in a single tournament it's easy – your target is to win the tournament. But if you're playing in a ring game, it's vital to know in advance both the maximum you're prepared to lose, and the amount you want to win, so that you can leave the game at the right time.

34

Play at the right level for your ability.

The temptation to move to a higher level before you're ready is always great, but it should be resisted. You must be consistently successful at the level you're playing at before you dip your toe in deeper financial waters.

35

If a player sits down at your table short-stacked – bully him.

He's made a fundamental poker error, and you should punish him. Raise him at every opportunity. Make it expensive for him even to enter a pot. His decision-making will be badly affected by his inadequate funds.

36

Be self-analytical. In particular, be honest with yourself about your areas of poker weakness. How can you improve if you won't admit that you've got any weaknesses in the first place?

37

Always **watch and remember** the face-up cards at **Seven Card Stud.** If you've got a pair, but one of the other two of that rank is face up on the table, your chances of hitting trips are immediately halved. If you're drawing to a flush, you need to know how many cards of your suit have already appeared on the table.

38

It can be very expensive to chase at Seven Card Stud. Occasionally the odds justify it, but some players play as though every hand is worth chasing. Your main strategy should be to play with big hands only, and let the others do the chasing against the odds.

39

Pay careful attention to every hand, even after you've folded.

A good technique is to 'ghost' the other players. Follow their moves and try to work out what you think they're holding, and what their strategy is. You will gain valuable insights into the way your table opponents play, and it will be much easier to get a read on them when you are in a hand with them.

40

You should **only ever play poker,**

whether online or in the casino,

when you're alert and ready to concentrate.

The single biggest reason that players lose money online is that they play when they are too tired (or worse, drunk) to play their best game. You can lose the whole of a hard won bankroll in a few minutes online if you're too tired to play.

41

In a home or casino game of poker, the easiest way to avoid giving tells to your opponents is to **keep a poker face.** It's not called that for nothing. If you try to be clever by acting or giving fake tells, you are likely to shoot yourself in the foot.

42

Watch the other players for tells. Especially look at your opponents' eyes. For example, a player in late position who glances at the opponents on his left is probably considering trying to steal the blinds.

43

A surprising number of **players** think it is clever to **behave as though they have the opposite hand** to the one they actually hold. For example, a player holding the nuts will frequently bet with a sigh, as though he's very reluctant to put his money down. If someone does this, you should usually fold unless you have strong evidence to the contrary.

44

Watch for tells from players who have already folded.

For example, if the flop comes 7-2-2, and someone pulls a face, he's quite probably folded 7-2. If there was a pre-flop raise, he may have folded a pair of sevens or even deuces. This can be valuable information if you're still in the hand.

45

When a player who has won a pot shows his hand when he doesn't have to, he is usually preparing to play with the opposite type of hand. So if he shows down a bluff, the next time he bets he will usually have the hand he is representing. If he shows a monster when he doesn't need to, he'll probably be bluffing some time soon.

46

If you're playing Omaha Hi/Lo

(also known as Omaha/8), remember that the lowest low hand is determined by the top card, not the bottom. So 76543 is lower than 8432A. And remember that only two cards from your hand can contribute to either the high or the low. Once you have fully grasped these two concepts, Omaha Hi/Lo is an excellent game to play online as so many players do not understand the rules!

47

In Omaha Hi/Lo, you should **consider folding any starting hand that does not contain an Ace.** This will save you lots of money, and ensure that when you are in a hand you have a realistic chance of winning, or at least splitting, the pot.

48

Don't bluff on the internet at low-limit poker.

There will always be someone who will call you. The main reason to bluff is so that you will get action when you really do have a hand. This just isn't a problem at low limits online. Fold your bad hands and wait for the good ones.

49

Keep a strict record of your poker sessions.

How much did you win or lose? How long did you play for? Were you playing Hold'em? Seven Card Stud? Limit or No-Limit? Tournament or ring game? You need this information, kept over a long period, to be able to analyse your level of success – or failure.

50

Recognize

when you're on tilt and stop playing immediately.

Everyone goes on tilt (loses their discipline completely) at some point. There's no shame in that – but there is in going on playing when you know you should stop. Get up and walk away from the table or switch off your computer.

Glossary

All-in When a player wages all his remaining chips in a single bet

Blind (small or big) Hands that are obliged to bet before the player has seen his cards

Board Community cards in Hold'em or Omaha

Button Marker denoting the nominal dealer

Call Match the previous bet

Cowboys Kings

Deuce Two

Flop The first three community cards in Hold'em or Omaha

Fold Throw away your hand, thus not risking any more chips but forfeiting any chance of winning the pot

Heads up Poker game between two players

Jacks up Two pairs, the higher of which is Jacks

Kicker The deciding card when two players have a pair of equal value

Nuts The best possible hand

Outs Cards which, if dealt, will improve your hand to win the pot

Overcard Card in the player's hand that is bigger than any of the community cards

Pat hand Hand in Draw Poker where the player does not draw any cards

Pot The collective value of all the bets in a hand

Raise Increase the previous bet

River The fifth and final community card to be dealt in Hold'em or Omaha

Rockets Aces

Suited Any two cards of the same suit

Tell A subconscious gesture that gives away the strength (or weakness) of a player's hand

Tilt Complete loss of discipline leading to wild and inaccurate play, usually following a piece of bad luck

Trips Three of a kind

Turn The fourth and penultimate community card to be dealt in Hold'em or Omaha

Peter French

Peter French is a bookshop owner, musican and self-taught poker player. He does win the occasional online tournament, but would also like to point out that he has lost money by failing to observe every single one of the tips in this book at one time or another. He is known in his friendly home game as 'Piranha', although he claims lthat this is ironic and that a more appropriate nickname would be 'Cuttlefish', or even 'Guppy'. He dedicates this book to his fellow players 'Hymie', 'The Octopus', and 'No-Nickname'.

THE LITTLE BOOK OF
BRIDGE
TIPS
PETER FRENCH

THE LITTLE BOOK OF
CHESS
TIPS
PETER FRENCH

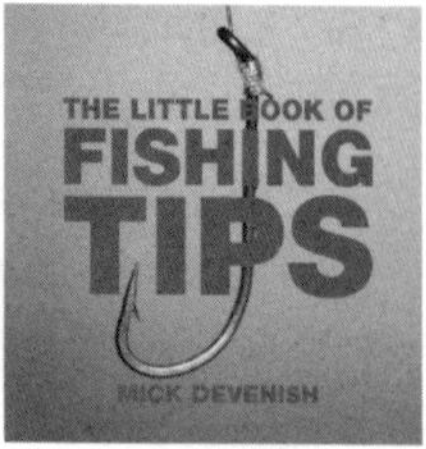
THE LITTLE BOOK OF
FISHING
TIPS
MICK DEVENISH

THE LITTLE BOOK OF
GREEN
TIPS
WILLIAM FORTT

THE LITTLE BOOK OF
KITTEN
TIPS
ANDREW LANGLEY

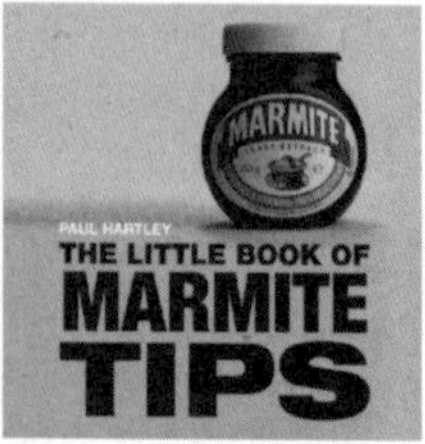
MARMITE
PAUL HARTLEY
THE LITTLE BOOK OF
MARMITE
TIPS

THE LITTLE BOOK OF
PUPPY
TIPS
ANDREW LANGLEY

THE LITTLE BOOK OF
WHISKY
TIPS
ANDREW LANGLEY

THE LITTLE BOOK OF
TRAVEL
TIPS
MEGAN DEVENISH

Little Books of Tips from Absolute Press

Aga Tips
Aga Tips 2
Aga Tips 3
Christmas Aga Tips
Rayburn Tips
Tea Tips
Coffee Tips
Wine Tips
Whisky Tips
Beer Tips
Cocktail Tips
Cheese Tips
Bread Tips
Herb Tips
Spice Tips
Curry Tips
Marmite Tips
Olive Oil Tips
Vinegar Tips
Pasta Tips
Cupcake Tips
Cake Decorating Tips
Macaroon Tips
Chocolate Tips
Ice Cream Tips
Chefs' Tips
Barbecue Tips
Gardening Tips
Houseplant Tips
Golf Tips
Travel Tips
Fishing Tips
Green Tips
Frugal Tips
Poker Tips
Bridge Tips
Chess Tips
Backgammon Tips
Scrabble Tips
Puppy Tips
Kitten Tips